MW00907232

KARDASHIAN'S QUOTES

Quotations of Kim, Khloe, Kourtney & Rob Kardashian, (Bruce) Caitlyn & Kris,Kendall Jenner, Lamar Odom, Kanye West

Table Of Content

Terms Of Use Agreement

Copyright 2015
All Rights Reserved

The author hereby asserts his/her right to be identified as the author of this work in accordance with sections 77 to 78 of the copyright, design and patents act 1988 as well as all other applicable international, federal, state and local laws.

Without limiting the rights under copyright reserved above, no part of this book may be reproduced, stored in or introduced into retrieval system, or transmitted, in any form or by any electronic or mechanical means, without the prior written permission of the copyright owner of this book, except by a reviewer who may quote brief passages.
There are no resale rights included. Anyone re - selling, or using this material in any way other than what is outlined within this book will be prosecuted to the full extend of the law.

Every effort had been made to fulfill requirements with regard to reproducing copyrighted material. The author and the publisher will be glad to certify any omissions at the earliest opportunity.

Disclaimer

The author and the publisher have used their best efforts in preparing this book. The author and the publisher make no representation or warranties with respect to the accuracy, fitness, applicability, or completeness of the contents of this work and specifically disclaim all warranties, including without limitation warranties of fitness for a particular purpose. This work is sold with the understanding that author and the publisher is not engaged in rendering legal, or any other professional services.

The information contained in this book is strictly for educational purposes. Therefore, if you wish to apply ideas contained within this book, you are taking full responsibility for your actions. The author and the publisher disclaim any warranties (express or implied), merchantability, or fitness for any particular purpose. The Author and The publisher shall in no event be held responsible / liable to any party for any indirect, direct, special, punitive, incidental, or other consequential damages arising directly or indirectly from any use of this material, which is provided 'as is', and without warranties.

The author and the publisher do not warrant the performance, applicability, or effectiveness of any websites and other medias listed or linked to in this publication. All links are for informative purposes only and are not warranted for contents, accuracy, or any other implied or explicit purpose.

Kim Kardashian

I don't even drink! I can't stand the taste of alcohol.
Every New Year's Eve I try one drink and every time it
makes me feel sick. So I don't touch booze - I'm always
the designated driver.
– Kim Kardashian

I always put clothes and family photos under the
mattress, in case the house burns down.
– Kim Kardashian

I always say you shouldn't weigh yourself. I don't even
have a set of scales in my house.
– Kim Kardashian

There was a time in my life where all I wanted was a
relationship, and I thought that was the most important
thing.
– Kim Kardashian

I am Armenian, so of course I am obsessed with laser
hair removal! Arms, bikini, legs, underarms... my entire
body is hairless.
– Kim Kardashian

To look and feel my best, I watch my calories and
exercise.
– Kim Kardashian

I'm an entrepreneur. 'Ambitious' is my middle name.
— Kim Kardashian

My decision to end my marriage was such a risk to lose ratings and lose my fan base. I had to take that risk for my inner peace and to be happy with myself.
— Kim Kardashian

There's more pressure to be famous for being yourself than if you're being a character.
— Kim Kardashian

I love when people underestimate me and then become pleasantly surprised.
— Kim Kardashian

I think if I'm 40 and I don't have any kids and I'm not married, I would have a baby artificially inseminated. I would feel like Mary - like Jesus is my baby.
— Kim Kardashian

I know people think we drive around in these nice cars and we do whatever we want and our parents will pay our credit cards, but that's not the case. Sure, my parents were generous; I got a nice car at 16, but at 18 I was cut off. I've worked really hard. I opened the store myself.
— Kim Kardashian

It's fun to have a partner who understands your life and lets you be you.
— Kim Kardashian

I promote a healthy lifestyle.
– Kim Kardashian

I couldn't sacrifice my heart for a publicity stunt.
– Kim Kardashian

I love the sun but don't have the time to get a good tan and keep it year-round, so I am a huge fan of tanning products.
– Kim Kardashian

I get letters from little girls begging me to adopt them.
– Kim Kardashian

You make mistakes, but I don't have any regrets. I'm the kind of person who takes responsibility for it and deals with it. I learn from everything I do. I work very hard, I have so many things going on in my life. Get to know me and see who I am.
– Kim Kardashian

Having lots of siblings is like having built-in best friends.
– Kim Kardashian

Maybe my fairy tale has a different ending than I dreamed it would. But that's OK.
– Kim Kardashian

When there's so many haters and negative things, I really don't care.
– Kim Kardashian

You never know what the future holds or where my life will take me.
– Kim Kardashian

People don't understand the pressure on me to look perfect.
– Kim Kardashian

I love meeting new people and telling them about my stories and my projects that I am working on.
– Kim Kardashian

My mom and I had the same vision, and we want the same things. We would always make a goal list every year.
– Kim Kardashian

I'm totally not against plastic surgery. I've tried Botox before. That's the only thing that I've done.
– Kim Kardashian

I hate to talk about myself.
– Kim Kardashian

I would rather have been beaten up in the media than live a life that wasn't happy.
– Kim Kardashian

Holidays are the best. I couldn't imagine being from a small family.
– Kim Kardashian

I have to be in a relationship in order to be intimate. I'm not the one-night-stand kind of girl. Despite the rumors.
– Kim Kardashian

I've made mistakes in my life for sure.
– Kim Kardashian

Personally, I've always loved the curvy look.
– Kim Kardashian

You can't really have like high end designers for everything.
– Kim Kardashian

I don't talk about money.
– Kim Kardashian

I am pretty honest about a lot of things that young girls question, like their body image.
– Kim Kardashian

People are recognizing that I am an entrepreneur and do more than be on a reality TV show.
– Kim Kardashian

The perfect date for me would be staying at home, making a big picnic in bed, eating Wotsits and cookies while watching cable TV.
– Kim Kardashian

It's time to recognise the Armenian Genocide.
– Kim Kardashian

If you're a basketball player and you don't stop and take pictures with your fans, you can have an amazing game and everyone still loves you.
– Kim Kardashian

Why is it when you're dieting, you crave everything?
– Kim Kardashian

I urge people to learn from the mistakes of others. Please drink responsibly and it's never acceptable to drink and drive!
– Kim Kardashian

When I gain a pound it's in the headlines.
– Kim Kardashian

I've always been the type to fall in love fast and, with every boyfriend, I plan out my wedding in my head.
– Kim Kardashian

I am fascinated by crime scene investigating. I swear, I wish I was a crime scene investigator sometimes!
– Kim Kardashian

I love to eat - Kit Kats or cookies-and-cream ice cream.
I need sugar like five times a day.
– Kim Kardashian

Now is the one time in my life I can be 100% selfish.
I'm not married; I don't have kids; I can focus on my
career.
– Kim Kardashian

I think you have different soulmates throughout your
life.
– Kim Kardashian

I was raised with a huge Armenian influence, always
hearing stories of Armenia, celebrating Armenian
holidays.
– Kim Kardashian

If I look at the message I'm portraying, I think it
definitely is be who you are, but be your best you.
– Kim Kardashian

I think each shoot has a different personality.
– Kim Kardashian

I've always been a businesswoman.
– Kim Kardashian

Botox to me is not surgery.
– Kim Kardashian

I am really cautious about what I say and do.
– Kim Kardashian

I went to college for four years.
– Kim Kardashian

I'd be foolish not to take some of these opportunities that are coming my way.
– Kim Kardashian

Even the people I surround myself with... are wiser, a little bit older than me, where before, all my boyfriends were younger.
– Kim Kardashian

Everything family does is reflection on the other people.
– Kim Kardashian

I definitely think anything I'd be in now is a permanent relationship.
– Kim Kardashian

I didn't love school.
– Kim Kardashian

I have cellulite, just like almost every other woman on the planet.
– Kim Kardashian

I just feel my best when I'm all glammed up.
– Kim Kardashian

I know some people say it's not the best to work with your family, but I have never understood that because it's always worked so well for me.
– Kim Kardashian

I love that my friends are sometimes even 20, 30 years older than me - that I can just sit and enjoy their company and their experiences.
– Kim Kardashian

I play into the perception of me, but it's not really me.
– Kim Kardashian

I will always believe in love, but my idea has changed from what I've always thought.
– Kim Kardashian

I am so stereotyped into being this Hollywood girl.
– Kim Kardashian

I definitely want kids and I want four kids, for sure. But I need to find a husband first!
– Kim Kardashian

I don't really have goals as far as, I want to be on a cover or something like that.
– Kim Kardashian

I was okay with school. My sister Kourtney was extremely smart. I always read a little slower.
– Kim Kardashian

I'm a little more shy and not comfortable dancing in front of a large crowd.
– Kim Kardashian

I'm totally growing up.
– Kim Kardashian

I'm the true definition of a workaholic.
– Kim Kardashian

White is actually one of my favorite colors. I have a white car. I love white.
– Kim Kardashian

I am hands-on in any project that I am associated with. I just don't want to put my face or name and lend it to a product that I'm not behind a hundred percent.
– Kim Kardashian

I remember when the wave of Jennifer Lopez, Salma Hayek and these beautiful Hispanic women came into light, and I looked up to them and I loved them, but I was like, 'Where are Middle Eastern women?'
– Kim Kardashian

I feel lazy when I'm not working. I learned all my business sense from my dad. He always believed in me, and I think the last thing he said to me before he passed away was, 'I know you're gonna be OK. I'm not worried about you'.
– Kim Kardashian

I always wanted what Mom and Dad had.
– Kim Kardashian

I have a hit TV show.
– Kim Kardashian

I wanted to be a teacher.
– Kim Kardashian

First and foremost, I married for love.
– Kim Kardashian

I can't dwell.
– Kim Kardashian

I feel like I'm at a really happy, good space.
– Kim Kardashian

I really see myself continuing to design clothes, fragrances.
– Kim Kardashian

I'm constantly on the go.
– Kim Kardashian

My reality is never going to be stick-skinny.
– Kim Kardashian

I was always really shy so I'd never try to get a guy's attention.
– Kim Kardashian

I do rely on having a full face on.
– Kim Kardashian

I have sister issues and parent issues and all sorts of things.
– Kim Kardashian

I learned how to cook and do a lot of marital things.
– Kim Kardashian

I think I'll always be a hopeless romantic.
– Kim Kardashian

I used to be super trendy and totally sexy. But I look back now and I used to want everything short and low cut and you really can't do it all.
– Kim Kardashian

I would absolutely characterize myself as ambitious.
– Kim Kardashian

If I like a food, I'll eat it, even if I know it's not good for me.
– Kim Kardashian

Maybe I'll just be a good aunt.
– Kim Kardashian

Me and my sisters all have such different body types.
– Kim Kardashian

My mother has always been the social glue holding the family together.
– Kim Kardashian

There are always going to be ridiculous rumours.
– Kim Kardashian

Khloe Kardashian Quotes

I don't think anybody should ever take their life for being bullied. But if it wasn't for my family... and my circle of friends, I could definitely see why someone would see it doesn't get any better than this, but it does. Life is so beautiful.
— Khloe Kardashian

I don't believe in revenge. When people are bullies it's because of a deeper-rooted issue - either their family life is tough or they're being bullied by someone bigger than they are.
— Khloe Kardashian

Not to be vain, but I have nice long legs, so I like to accentuate them. Find what part of your body you love most - it can be your arms, your chest, your legs - and emphasize that.
— Khloe Kardashian

I'm proud of myself. I could break and go get all this plastic surgery and get my nose fixed and get lipo or do whatever, but I haven't chosen to do that because I know I'm a great person. I'm pretty damn hot, if you ask me.
— Khloe Kardashian

Leopard print has been my thing forever! When I was a teenager my entire room was done in leopard print - it's

timeless, chic, and always in style. When in doubt...
leopard!
– Khloe Kardashian

A few years ago I lost 30 pounds, and people still
wanted to criticize. And honestly, I'm happy with myself
if I'm a little heavier. I realized: 'Why am I trying to
conform to someone else's idea of beauty?' I think I'm
beautiful either way.
– Khloe Kardashian

Now we have so many more social outlets, so many
ways to be stalked and bullied. If social media is too
much for you to handle, then don't have a Twitter or
Facebook account. Just be yourself. Be who you want to
be.
– Khloe Kardashian

But I also enjoy life... the more scrutiny I am under, the
more confident I become. I am who I am. I can't do
anything about it, and I love who I am.
– Khloe Kardashian

I'm thrilled to continue my partnership with U by Kotex
for Generation Know while helping to empower girls.
I've always been a motivational resource for my
younger sisters and hope I can positively impact and
inspire other young girls too.
– Khloe Kardashian

I have moments of weakness, but mostly I brush the criticism off... Who cares if I'm not a size zero? I don't want to be. I love my body; I'm healthy, I work out.
— Khloe Kardashian

I'm Armenian, but I'm very fair and I look white... I would always get such hate about it.
— Khloe Kardashian

I just think that knowing about your body at any age, whether it's educating yourself on fertility, getting mammograms, going through puberty - whatever it may be, is really important. I just really encourage women empowerment and being comfortable talking about these issues.
— Khloe Kardashian

My weight fluctuates, like any normal girl, and I have times when I feel insecure.
— Khloe Kardashian

I don't feel the pressure by outsiders. I'm not someone who's easily influenced by the public.
— Khloe Kardashian

I have two younger sisters and I'm such an advocate of owning who you are as a person. Don't be ashamed or intimidated. Never feel like you are not amazing.
— Khloe Kardashian

The Armenian Genocide is such a controversial and very sensitive issue because the Turkish and Armenian

people disagree about the facts of what actually happened. I know how strongly Armenians feel about the Genocide, and how it's never been recognised. At the same time, I do not hold today's generation of people accountable.
– Khloe Kardashian

You can't expect everyone to love you. I'm not someone who just wants to throw out hate, just because.
– Khloe Kardashian

I'm not shy about wearing a lot of makeup! But when I don't have to be done up, I just use a bit of concealer and maybe some lip balm.
– Khloe Kardashian

I'm strong and fearless and not afraid to take risks in business.
– Khloe Kardashian

I live in a world where there's magazines and blogs, and people feel like they are allowed to criticize me, and in the meanest way.
– Khloe Kardashian

Fame comes and fame goes, but you have to be able to laugh about yourself and to take it with a grain of salt.
– Khloe Kardashian

I don't think because I hang out with enough black people, I'm gonna turn black. What kind of

rationalization is that? I'm just friends with people that I like. I don't care what skin color you are.
– Khloe Kardashian

I just let my hair go - if there's no hairdresser around I really can't be bothered!
– Khloe Kardashian

I used to follow trends and try to do exactly what I saw in the magazines, but I'm not a Victoria's Secret model who can wear anything.
– Khloe Kardashian

I went to Catholic school and they basically just said don't have sex, but would never explain anything.
– Khloe Kardashian

People make me feel like I have a problem because I haven't had a kid yet.
– Khloe Kardashian

The bikini waxing, after we go there you can't turn back.
– Khloe Kardashian

A lot of adults don't think it's their place to interfere with kids. I interfere all the time.
– Khloe Kardashian

Part of being married is knowing when your husband needs your support.
– Khloe Kardashian

One of the biggest struggles of my life is my weight. My weight is always going up and down, and I'm always fighting that, and I think that no matter what I do, I'm never going to look good enough to everybody else.
– Khloe Kardashian

I'm the ugly sister. I'm the fat one. I'm the transvestite. I have had those mean things said about me at least twice a day for the last five years. It's horrible, you know? But I can brush that stuff off.
– Khloe Kardashian

My father raised us like... we were not allowed to see people in any sort of colors, but also we were not allowed to call people fat. If ever we were to say, 'Oh that fat person, or this person,' he would make us put a bar of soap in our mouth and count to 10. We weren't allowed to look at people like that.
– Khloe Kardashian

We're all our own worst critics and so hard on ourselves, but for me, my biggest insecurity is my arms. I just hate the tops of them. I work out and they still never look good enough for me. So, over the years I've learned to dress to make myself feel better.
– Khloe Kardashian

I like to do designs on the side of my face, or cut out foil stickers from the crafts store and put them on my forehead.
– Khloe Kardashian

My hubby is such a sneaker king... and I am a stiletto queen! He always wants to see me in sneakers, but I believe I can do anything in heels.
– Khloe Kardashian

To be able to design for the plus-sized consumer, for me, that's just beyond. It's a dream.
– Khloe Kardashian

Everyone expects me to be 9 feet tall and weigh 200 pounds when they meet me.
– Khloe Kardashian

I am an organization freak!
– Khloe Kardashian

I'm not really an actress.
– Khloe Kardashian

I'm so excited. I love radio and being on the new Mix 102.9.
– Khloe Kardashian

When I did the cover of 'Cosmo International,' Turkey picked it up and I got a lot of backlash for it.
– Khloe Kardashian

I always have mini bottles of Unbreakable, the fragrance I did with my husband. I'm Armenian, so I'm oily and always have blotting papers.
– Khloe Kardashian

I love doing fashion.
– Khloe Kardashian

I say all the time I think there should be some courses in the regular schooling system that isn't, even like about credit, things that matter later in life. I learned the harder way: 'Look, I got a $500 credit card in the mail, let's go shopping!'
– Khloe Kardashian

I've had a lot of really influential people in my life, like my grandmother M. J., who have helped me along the way. But there are so many of us girls in my family, and even though they're all so open and honest, who I seek advice from depends on what aspect of life I'm dealing with.
– Khloe Kardashian

If I'm cooking dinner for my hubby or designing a line or selling on QVC, I try to do it in an authentic way. To speak to people like I want to be spoken to, to be a voice for people who don't have one and to give them things they need and love.
– Khloe Kardashian

We come from a very mixed family. We're a bunch of different races, my family. So it's very normal for us. I don't know why we're accepted. Are all of us accepted or just me?
– Khloe Kardashian

I love all of my shoes! It is a must to have them color coordinated, and to be able to see each and every one of them. I know exactly where each one lives and I can tell if one has even been moved!
– Khloe Kardashian

It's easier to date a football player for sure. Football players have one game a week, and they practice every day, but they're all at home. In basketball, they're on the road all the time.
– Khloe Kardashian

When I was at home, I felt loved and safe. My sisters were always a safe haven for me. I knew they would always play with me and make me feel like I was one of them.
– Khloe Kardashian

I'm not big on looking up myself. I don't get Google alerts, and I don't look on blogs.
– Khloe Kardashian

I'm a modern girl, but you should put your husband first. I like to think divorce is not an option.
– Khloe Kardashian

If I want to wear a long flowing dress, someone will say I'm pregnant.
– Khloe Kardashian

If you're too embarrassed and want to hide behind your computer screen, that's what this is for. It's about

building confidence and that's what U by Kotex does.
Girls owning their bodies and health.
– Khloe Kardashian

Kourtney Kardashian Quotes

I remember, when I went away to college at Southern Methodist University in Dallas, my aunt sent me a book with the rules of being a Southern Belle. One of the rules was to never wear white after Labor Day. Fashion has a lot to do with confidence and making up your own rules.
– Kourtney Kardashian

I would say a lack of sleep is a cause for feeling not so beautiful. On those days, I try to drink lots of water and put on the biggest sunglasses I can find.
– Kourtney Kardashian

Motherhood has most definitely changed me and my life. It's so crazy how drastic even the small details change - in such an amazing way. Even silly things, like the fact that all of my pictures on my cell phone used to be of me at photo shoots - conceited, I know! - but now every single picture on my phone is of Mason.
– Kourtney Kardashian

I loved dressing for my pregnant body. A pregnant woman's body is so beautiful. Towards the end, it does get harder, and then it became all about flats and comfortable maxi dresses.
– Kourtney Kardashian

Being a mom is what life is about. I hope people realize what the priorities in life should be and know not everything has to be perfect.
– Kourtney Kardashian

I've been wearing lipstick since I was in 7th grade. That was our form of daring self-expression, because we had to wear uniforms in school. It made our teachers so angry.
– Kourtney Kardashian

There's no one else I would rather have as my manager than my mom because I know that she has our best interests at heart. Sometimes, it's hard to separate manager mode from mom mode. I think as our manager, my mom will get more emotional about situations than she would if she was just our manager.
– Kourtney Kardashian

I know that, for me, I need to try to cover myself while breastfeeding so that no one snaps a picture. If this wasn't the case, I probably wouldn't mind as much because my son is my biggest concern. My attitude is, if someone sees a little somethin' somethin', don't look if you don't like it.
– Kourtney Kardashian

Fashion is so subjective, and I think it should be playful.
– Kourtney Kardashian

For me, juggling mommy hood and work is a challenge, but each day I learn little tricks to make it all come together.
– Kourtney Kardashian

I love Audrey Hepburn.
– Kourtney Kardashian

Sometimes I think, 'Why should I work out when I can spend time with my kids?' I feel guilty doing something for me.
– Kourtney Kardashian

When every moment is constantly being filmed, it's hard to relax.
– Kourtney Kardashian

Sometimes I just wish nobody knew who I was.
– Kourtney Kardashian

Growing up, I never heard my parents curse, never. The first time I ever said a curse word was with my sister Kim.
– Kourtney Kardashian

I think motherhood is just about instinct. I remember coming home from the hospital and having no idea what we were doing.
– Kourtney Kardashian

I'm proof that, even after having a baby, you can look better and sexier than ever!
– Kourtney Kardashian

People always have something to say about how long is too long or not long enough to breastfeed. I think this is such a personal decision that it can only be made between each baby and his or her mommy.
– Kourtney Kardashian

I have so many pieces that once belonged to my mom and both of my grandmothers. All of these pieces are very sentimental, and I love to wear them. I also have many pieces from my father that I probably cherish the most. I love wearing his dress shirts.
– Kourtney Kardashian

I used to play Donna Karan. I used my dad's home office, and Kim was my assistant. Then one of our friends would play a buyer, and I would take her to my mom's closet and show her the new collection.
– Kourtney Kardashian

I'm five feet tall - I'm very petite - so for me, if I'm wearing a skirt or dress, it needs to be short, or else it makes me look frumpy. I need to wear either something really short or a maxi dress; anything in between just looks weird.
– Kourtney Kardashian

I feel such a sense of empowerment being a mom. But I do wonder: How do they/we do it all?
– Kourtney Kardashian

I feel that if I'm going through something, I'm sure someone else is, too. I try to be as honest with myself and others as I can be.
– Kourtney Kardashian

I love Oreos.
– Kourtney Kardashian

I think it's important to talk to my sisters when I have a big decision to make.
– Kourtney Kardashian

I wish that when we weren't filming, we could have full privacy. I wish I could live in a bubble and just be with my family.
– Kourtney Kardashian

I am the worst at doing my hair. I have no clue how to do it; I just feel like I need to go to hair beauty school or something because it's really becoming a problem.
– Kourtney Kardashian

I would love to design a maternity clothing line. It is so hard to find stylish clothes for pregnant people... I would say 99 percent of the clothes I wore were not maternity because I couldn't find anything I liked.
– Kourtney Kardashian

My best friend and I went to sleep-away camp every summer. We'd share stories of making out with boys, but we never did, so we made it all up. My real first kiss was at a friend's house when I was in junior high. He was such a good kisser, and we're still close friends!
– Kourtney Kardashian

I have had breast implants, but it's so funny 'cause it's not a secret; I could care less.
– Kourtney Kardashian

I love to read books that focus on parenting topics because there are so many different ways to do things. I find these books offer a lot of great opinions on many different subjects.
– Kourtney Kardashian

When I was pregnant, a few of my friends told me that their babies slept in bed with them. I remember thinking how crazy that was. Then I started reading up on it and decided it was something I actually wanted to try.
– Kourtney Kardashian

I don't think anyone can fall in love for ratings.
– Kourtney Kardashian

My step dad is Bruce Jenner, the Olympian. The first time he came over was like a blind date, and we had show and tell. He took out the gold medal for me and

my sisters, and we were like, 'So? Who the hell are you?'
– Kourtney Kardashian

I think with boys... it's all about shoes. I've seen so many little boys, and their outfits are so cute, and then their moms put kind of dorky shoes on them.
– Kourtney Kardashian

Now that I have a daughter, I've been thinking about how I'll define beauty to her. I watched a video of Kendall when she was three, and she was putting on makeup. I don't know how I feel about that. But my daughter already watches me do it. When do you let them start wearing it? I don't know yet.
– Kourtney Kardashian

Rob Kardashian Quotes

I am working on a dress sock line of funky, colorful, cool designs.
– Rob Kardashian

I feel like dress socks differentiate you in a different way - especially men in suits who just have the traditional business suit. The dress sock is the way to change it up in your mind and I like wearing my pants up higher so you see them.
– Rob Kardashian

I literally change my phone number 10 times a year and I don't ever save my contacts.
– Rob Kardashian

I want to experience Dallas. It's a new city where I see new business opportunities.
– Rob Kardashian

If I could be anyone, I'd choose the lead singer of Arcade Fire, Win Butler.
– Rob Kardashian

I'm obsessed with neon sneakers.
– Rob Kardashian

No one wants to see a boring tube sock.
– Rob Kardashian

I feel like more than 80% of the world wouldn't get up in front of 40 million people and dance on national television, and if I have the confidence to do that then that's a step ahead in my life for me in terms of personal goals. I will gain a lot of confidence on all aspects right there.
– Rob Kardashian

I sleep with my baby blanket, Kiki, that my nana made for me.
– Rob Kardashian

I'm a Pisces - emotional.
– Rob Kardashian

(Bruice) Caitlyn Jenner Quotes

Probably a mistake I made was maybe not having her understand — not the severity of it but that this is a condition you cannot get away from. From that standpoint maybe I blew it away a little bit, sort of 'This is what I do.'
– Caitlyn Jenner - On misleading Kris

The first 15 years I felt she needed me more because I was the breadwinner . . . then really around the show, when that hit and she was running this whole show and getting credit for it and she had her own money, she didn't need me from that standpoint. The relationship was different.
– Caitlyn Jenner - About his marriage to Kris

A lot of times she (Kris) wasn't very nice, people would see how I got mistreated. She controlled the money . . . all that kind of stuff
– Caitlyn Jenner

Twenty percent was gender and 80 percent was the way I was treated.
– Caitlyn Jenner - About divorce

If I wasn't dyslexic, I probably wouldn't have won the Games. If I had been a better reader, then that would have come easily, sports would have come easily... and

I never would have realized that the way you get ahead in life is hard work.
– Caitlyn Jenner

First of all, I try to be a positive role model.
– Caitlyn Jenner

The biggest problem with dyslexic kids is not the perceptual problem, it is their perception of themselves. That was my biggest problem.
– Caitlyn Jenner

I am from the Kardashian group. We can take anything.
– Caitlyn Jenner

I always felt that my greatest asset was not my physical ability, it was my mental ability.
– Caitlyn Jenner

I always thought everybody else was better than me.
– Caitlyn Jenner

I spent twelve years training for a career that was over in a week. Joe Namath spent one week training for a career that lasted twelve years.
– Caitlyn Jenner

If I had not been dyslexic, I wouldn't have needed sports. I would have been like every other kid. Instead,

I found my one thing, and I was never going to let go of it. That little dyslexic kid is always in the back of your head.
– Caitlyn Jenner

I thought everybody else was doing much better than I was.
– Caitlyn Jenner

If you're asking your kids to exercise, then you better do it, too. Practice what you preach.
– Caitlyn Jenner

If you're going to dedicate every second to winning the decathlon, what are you doing wasting your time in bed?
– Caitlyn Jenner

It's about working when nobody's watching.
– Caitlyn Jenner

Start early and begin raising the bar throughout the day.
– Caitlyn Jenner

I didn't only have a perceptual problem, I was also so nervous and so upset. The process just didn't work. I lost enthusiasm for school and I flunked second grade. The teachers said I was lazy.
– Caitlyn Jenner

I still have nightmares about taking tests.
– Caitlyn Jenner

I was growing up in the 50's and 60's. Back then they didn't even know what dyslexia was.
– Caitlyn Jenner

If you are dyslexic, your eyes work fine, your brain works fine, but there is a little short circuit in the wire that goes between the eye and the brain. Reading is not a fluid process.
– Caitlyn Jenner

Waving the flag at the 1976 Olympics wasn't my idea. It was too much apple pie and ice cream. Not that I don't love my country, but I felt it was my victory up there, I put all the time into it.
– Caitlyn Jenner

If you are a kid, reading is really important stuff.
– Caitlyn Jenner

Our mission for younger people is to do our best to make exercise cool, hip - the thing to do.
– Caitlyn Jenner

It caused more problems as a young kid, because the simple process of perceiving words on a piece of paper was hard for me. Many people think dyslexic people see things backwards. They don't see things backwards.
– Caitlyn Jenner

I was a dyslexic kid.
– Caitlyn Jenner

Nobody has milked one performance better than me -
and I'm damned proud of it.
– Caitlyn Jenner

We put so much pressure on kids to excel in school at
such a young age.
– Caitlyn Jenner

That's the most important thing you do in your life -
raise children and try to do the best job as a parent and
give your kids the best shot in life to go out there into
the big, bad world.
– Caitlyn Jenner

The truth is everybody does it from time to time. People
dial telephone numbers and they get a wrong number
only to find that they've read the last two digits
backwards. Everybody does it, but dyslexics have this
tendency to a higher degree.
– Caitlyn Jenner

Kris Jenner Quotes

If somebody says 'no', you're asking the wrong person.
— Kris Jenner, Kris Jenner

When you feel like something's really wrong, it's usually
wrong
— Kris Jenner

It's often said that life's a dance, and I am continually
learning new steps
— Kris Jenner

I know we will live longer and happier lives with a
passion and a purpose
— Kris Jenner

You are going to meet the same people on the way
down as you did on the way up. So be grateful and
humble for the blessings that have been given to you.
— Kris Jenner

This is what being a mom means: unconditional, all of
the time.
— Kris Jenner

Like the famous lady in the frame (Mona Lisa), to many
we remain a mystery
— Kris Jenner

You have to understand that relationships have their ebbs and flows, and that life just evolves. It is about love and friendship. It not always about passion and heat. I just didn't understand that.
— Kris Jenner

I represent all of my kids...but if I took on Brandon and Leah, it would be so much pressure...it would kill me if I made a wrong decision.
– Kris Jenner

The opportunity to work with my family and just knowing that we got to get up every day and be together and have some fun. Were having a really good time and were passionate about it. What meant the most to me was that I got to be with the kids.
– Kris Jenner

Thank you. A girl never knows when she might need a couple of diamonds at ten 'o' clock in the morning.
– Kris Jenner

Thats just how my intuition kicks in. After finishing the first season, we went right into season two, so we really didnt have a break. Everything happened so fast. I love business and I love what I'm doing. When youre really passionate about something and something fits, you just roll with that.
– Kris Jenner

Everything we go after or that comes to us, we just say 'Is this something that we love? Is this something that

we would use or that we would wear? And is this something we can really put our stamp on?' The girls love the fact that they design their own clothing line. Its an exciting thing to be able to do. I love my clothing line. We spend a lot of time all year long designing and picking out fabrics and styles and buttons and zippers. When you love something that much it comes really easily, it's just a natural. If something doesn't feel good and it's a struggle and it's just something that we don't like, then it wouldn't be anything we could put our name on.
– Kris Jenner

Kim is so great at her social media. The whole family interacts with the fans. Things are so instantaneous and we enjoy Facebook, Twitter and our blogs. It's a great way of letting people know what we're up to.
– Kris Jenner

I'm here in Las Vegas judging the Miss America competition and I have a blog about winning tickets sweepstakes, and people are tweeting about the kind of core values they think that the new Miss America should have. We just let people know what's going on in our lives. If we have a new product coming out, we can let our audience know about that. We can give friends and family members support using Twitter or let people know if something is going on in the world or where we are and what were experiencing. It's enjoyable, informational, and it really drives our fan base.
– Kris Jenner

It's just one day at a time. I love multi-tasking and I'm really organized and when you have a certain work ethic, which all the girls have, we all have that same thing going on.
– Kris Jenner

I just sharted myself. That's when you fart and you shit yourself on accident!
– Kris Jenner

Some idiot hacking my phone in the middle of night to listen to my messages. Hey Sherlock! Nice try but please don't erase them anymore!
– Kris Jenner

It's annoying when I hear, What do your girls do? Well, first of all, all of my daughters have jobs. They are fashion stylists and designers; they own a chain of stores. They had the stores before they had the show. And my kids worked from the time they were 13 years old. So to me, that's a huge misconception, that the girls don't work. They work 25 hours a day.
– Kris Jenner

I think Khloe has taken a stand on it over the years, I don't want to ever hurt anyone else's feelings or tread on anyone else's privacy or make anyone feel bad, so if I do I'm the first one to say 'I'm sorry, I didn't really mean that' and I teach my kids the same thing.
– Kris Jenner

Kim, Kourtney, Khloe and Rob, we all have pretty tough skin. If someone feels like they need to take a shot, well okay. It's not going to change our life...But honestly every single day we have the last laugh because we are having so much damn fun.
– Kris Jenner

You can either be a problem maker or a problem solver. And I'm a problem solver.
– Kris Jenner

Anytime you hurt somebody else it's definitely just tragic...To ruin someone else's self-esteem or make someone feel bad about anything is never right.
– Kris Jenner

From a young age I made fashion very important and at the same time lots of fun. I feel life is fabulous and live it out loud. Fashion is an extension of who we are, whether shopping at Chanel or Target!
– Kris Jenner

You must start with great hair and makeup whether you do it yourself or not and everything else will fall into place. I think keeping it simple these days, and most of all comfortable, you will have a really great time!
– Kris Jenner

My girls' work ethic is second to none. They get up at 4 a.m., go to work, work until they fall down, and then get up the next day and do it all over again.
– Kris Jenner

From a young age, I taught them about waxing and mani-pedis, and we always made it a party!
– Kris Jenner

He was married to me and he wasn't who he wanted to be so he was miserable . . . All I was doing was working very hard for my family so that we could all have a wonderful future, and he was pissed off. At the end of my relationship with Bruce he definitely had a lot of social anxiety. That was one of the reasons we were in a struggle at the end. We fought a lot because we would go out together and before we got to the end of the block we were in a fight because he started saying 'when can we go home?'
– Kris Jenner - On Bruce

Why would you want to be married and have kids if this is what you wanted since you were a little boy. Why would you not explain this all to me?
– Kris Jenner - On Caitlin

When I met Bruce he told me that he had done hormones back in the early 80s. This was a conversation that took place in the early 90s. So, what he was telling me happened a decade earlier, and he never really explained it. There wasn't a gender issue. Nobody mentioned a gender issue. Somebody mentioned that at one point in his life [he] liked to dress up.
– Kris Jenner

I did my boobs in 1988. That was almost like it didn't count because it was something I felt I had to do after having four kids. My boobs were kind of shot.
– Kris Jenner

Kendall Jenner Quotes

Modeling is my number one priority - one hundred percent.
– Kendall Jenner

What people don't understand is that calling someone too skinny is the same as calling someone too fat; it's not a nice feeling.
– Kendall Jenner

My name is Kendall. – Kendall Jenner. I am not a Kardashian.
– Kendall Jenner

My ideal prom date would have to be cute, funny, sweet, nice.
– Kendall Jenner

Me and Kylie are sisters, but not everything we can always do together. She's not trying to be a model. She's trying to be more like a personality. We're trying to kind of separate ourselves - not in a bad way!
– Kendall Jenner

It's true, I used to be so shy. I used to never talk, just sit back and do my thing. I was never bullied, though, and it was never like it was something that needed to be 'fixed', like being shy is a bad thing.
– Kendall Jenner

Ask me a question about paparazzi, and I get so heated. And I feel so bad for young kids of celebrities. My nieces and nephews get yelled at, and I'm like, 'You are yelling at a 2-year-old.'
– Kendall Jenner

My favorite thing about doing photo shoots is just being able to have fun, meeting new people, getting dressed up, and I just love doing it. So, I have a lot of fun.
– Kendall Jenner

I'm lucky that I've never been bullied personally. There are always going to be kids who are mean and say stuff, but the people that matter to you - the people you love, like your parents, your siblings, and your friends - those are the people you should listen to.
– Kendall Jenner

Sometimes I just want to be left alone and be a normal kid for, like, five minutes. That's tough when the paparazzi are chasing you.
– Kendall Jenner

I want to continue modeling and do the best that I can with that.
– Kendall Jenner

I definitely want to design clothes at one point.
– Kendall Jenner

The New York fashion scene is crazy, madness, but I love the energy.
– Kendall Jenner

I'm a very loyal and very private person when it comes to my personal life. But I obviously do have Twitter and Instagram, and I will share some of the things I'm doing.
– Kendall Jenner

In first grade, I told my friends I had a third story in my house filled with jewels and lions.
– Kendall Jenner

I guess my style's a little edgy but comfortable. I like being comfortable, for sure, and kind of casual.
– Kendall Jenner

I don't work with a trainer. I just go to cheer leading practice and run a couple times a week.
– Kendall Jenner

I volunteered at Meals on Wheels, which is a place where you go and deliver healthy meals to people who are more home bound. I did that, and I had so much fun doing it, and I'm definitely planning on doing it again.
– Kendall Jenner

I'm obsessed with Tumblr. I love looking at all the pictures!
– Kendall Jenner

If I see something really nasty on Twitter, I will usually delete it or block the person because I don't want to see that every day... Get to know me, and then you can talk about me!
– Kendall Jenner

I think mascara is a must. If I'm going to wear makeup somewhere, and I'm doing it, it's usually really simple - it's just mascara and maybe a tiny bit of eyeshadow, but that's it.
– Kendall Jenner

I'm trying my best with what I want to do, which is modelling. I think I'm on my own career path, and I don't really care what other people have to say about me being in the spotlight of my sisters. I'm just doing my own thing.
– Kendall Jenner

If I could trade places with any of my sisters for a day, it would be Kim. I want to see what it's like... The only time she sleeps is on the airplane. It's just crazy. I feel bad for her, but I still want to know what it's like.
– Kendall Jenner

My way to de-stress is either listening to music or talking to my sister, Kourtney. She's going to teach me how to meditate, and that should help a lot.
– Kendall Jenner

My style icon actually is my three sisters. I love the way they dress and the way they put things together. I definitely get most of my style from them.
– Kendall Jenner

I really don't have a celebrity crush.
– Kendall Jenner

My dream jobs would be Italian 'Vogue' and anything with Chanel!
– Kendall Jenner

Lamar Odom Quotes

It could have been called a foul. But if it's not, I guess that means I just didn't go hard enough. I thought it was a tough move.
– Lamar Odom

When you play good defense, you give yourself opportunities to beat teams. When you play bad defense, you give yourself opportunities to lose to any team.
– Lamar Odom

I put Kobe in a bind out there. He has to score 40 points just for us to win. I don't blame him for shooting 40 shots some nights. We should be embarrassed as a team. I know I am.
– Lamar Odom

We don't know how to win ugly yet. It's either we have good offensive games or we lose.
– Lamar Odom

The third quarter is really biting us in the butt. It's a team defensive thing we've just got to fix.
– Lamar Odom

The time off was good for the mind and body. I was just more aggressive tonight.
– Lamar Odom

I kept myself in the game by rebounding the ball. There's a lot of ways I can help this team. I just got to play good basketball, be smart with the basketball.
– Lamar Odom

That's going to be his place in history. Right now, he's really focused and feels like it's his league. Before the 81 points, Kobe should have been getting his due as far as the MVP.
– Lamar Odom

So now that we go back home we've got to find a way to keep our ship afloat. In the second half of the season, every game is going to be towards gaining some playoff position.
– Lamar Odom

Kobe, he has really strong will. When he's in the zone like that, he's definitely on an island by himself.
– Lamar Odom

My man is feeling it. He's got it cooking.
– Lamar Odom

I'm kind of lost for words. It was a pleasure just to watch him out here.
– Lamar Odom

Kobe helps me too, because if I'm ever lying back too much, him trying to get open or him fighting wakes me up. Kobe's game is like smelling salts. If you're lying

back, he's going to get you up. He's the best player I've
ever played with.
– Lamar Odom

Kobe helps me too, because if I'm ever lying back too
much, him trying to get open or him fighting wakes me
up, ... Kobe's game is like smelling salts. If you're lying
back, he's going to get you up. He's the best player I've
ever played with.
– Lamar Odom

The Lakers' weakness in the paint isn't lost on the
team.] It's my job to take some pressure off [Bryant]
as far as making plays, ... I wasn't able to do that
tonight. That won't cut it. I've got to find a way to
become a little more assertive.
– Lamar Odom

Right now you have a lot of power forwards who have
small-forward athleticism and abilities,
– Lamar Odom

Without our best offensive player, we've got to play
better defense.
– Lamar Odom

Kirilenko must have thought he was in Salt Lake City
tonight. A couple of times he made tough shots.
– Lamar Odom

If this were football, I would be listed as probable.
– Lamar Odom

I got home, and my son told me how much he loved watching Kobe. We're playing with somebody who's making history as he goes along. It's like traveling with a rock star.
– Lamar Odom

This should be a confidence-booster for our team, especially after the game last night.
– Lamar Odom

It's like God put Kobe here for us to watch him play basketball.
– Lamar Odom

We've got to make every game a defensive game. ... When you play the worst defensive game of the year, you get beat. Point blank.
– Lamar Odom

His mouth is horrible and atrocious.
– Lamar Odom

His ability is amazing, and his will is amazing.
– Lamar Odom

That's just the way he is. He's always been that way.
– Lamar Odom

We get to have a light practice, lift a little weights, have a steak and relax a little bit.
– Lamar Odom

This is a big road trip for us. We want to go in there [tonight], and it'd be a good time to play your best game of the year so we could keep it going a little bit.
– Lamar Odom

He's the best rookie I've every played with. He just makes plays. He's not getting a lot of hype right now, but people are going to find out about Mr. Wade.
– Lamar Odom

We'll do it. If we have to do it, we'll certainly do it.
– Lamar Odom

We played poorly. That's just what you expect.
– Lamar Odom

It's a blessing to be out on the court with him, and tonight he showed why, again. It's crazy. Eighty-one points, that's a lot of points. A lot of players couldn't do that because they would just let up. It's a testament to his will, really. It's so strong. He's a strong-minded dude.
– Lamar Odom

I'm not scared to shoot it.
– Lamar Odom

That was a great move. He's real athletic, so you can just throw the ball by the rim and he'll go up and finish it. We're trying to find him. He's real aggressive

underneath the basket. He's protecting our paint, and we love the job that he's doing.
– Lamar Odom

This was not like having a cold or the flu, this was a complicated surgery. Some people lose their lives, not just their career. When you figure he's been able to play for us, and even to be effective for us, anybody has to be inspired. He's defeated some long odds to be here and now he's an emotional part of this team.
– Lamar Odom

The hip-hop culture is part of the NBA, ... It's not going to leave just because we change what we wear.
– Lamar Odom

This group is a little bit closer because we've been together since training camp,
– Lamar Odom

Some games you have to do the right thing basketball-wise to win and we can't seem to do that. We don't play a good offensive game and we can't win. That puts Kobe in a bind. He's got to get 35 or 40 points for us to win. We should be embarrassed. I know I am.
– Lamar Odom

When we were down at halftime, (Bryant) was ticked. He said nothing and that was scary.
– Lamar Odom

We just threw everybody at (Pierce). If you put two guys on him, you have a high percentage of stopping him.
– Lamar Odom

We needed this game, so I just wanted to stay aggressive around the boards, find the basket, get some easy shots and go to the free throw line.
– Lamar Odom

We played a great defensive game against Detroit, a great defensive game against Oklahoma (New Orleans) and San Antonio, and we do the little things that it takes to win big games. Then we come back tonight and we just don't scrap enough. I don't know if that's youth. I don't know if it's a heart thing. I hope it's not a heart thing.
– Lamar Odom

Once he learns how to settle in ... he will be all right. I try to tell him sometimes go easy and pick your spots ... jab, jab, jab and then hook. But with him right now it's like hook, hook, hook, hook. But he is a great offensive player. He might get the start.
– Lamar Odom

He's very patient, ... He takes his time with us. He's what you call a team player right now.
Author: Odom Quotes Category: None

We're over it. Everybody's over it in this organization. (Nuggets fans) should have been over it. (It) didn't

happen to them. I don't know why they take it so personally.
– Lamar Odom

He was a good dude before. He's an even better dude now. This is a guy who's been through a lot. He's one guy who knows how fragile life can be.
– Lamar Odom

He's one of the best small forwards ever. You could argue he's the best, although I'll bet you James Worthy would probably have a good argument about that. But he's an all-around player. And I consider myself to be an all-around player.
– Lamar Odom

We're not going to get caught up playing their game. We're going to execute offensively. We're going to make them beat us. We're not going to give them the game.
– Lamar Odom

Different tricks of the trade, different ways to get open, different ways to play defense, different ways to play the game. He knows the triangle inside-out.
– Lamar Odom

It sounds good, something like that.
– Lamar Odom

I think we're not trusting one another offensively and defensively.

– Lamar Odom

I'm disappointed to hear that because he's my friend.
Sometimes, we tend to do things at the spur of the
moment that we wish we could take back because it
hurts our image. But I'm pretty sure he was just a little
upset emotionally because they were playing the
Clippers.
– Lamar Odom

We dug ourselves a hole. We can't afford to go 18 down
and expect to win.
– Lamar Odom

I like Odom as a player, but I don't know if I'd trust
him.
– Lamar Odom

We didn't protect each other. I actually had to go to an
enforcer style, and that's not my game. We were just
really bad on team defense.
– Lamar Odom

We didn't protect each other, ... I actually had to go to
an enforcer style, and that's not my game. We were
just really bad on team defense.
– Lamar Odom

I think that's the strength to my game. I'm not
one-dimensional at all. I'm comfortable wherever he
wants me to play on the court. I kind of pride myself
being able to play any position. Anything to help us

create mismatches, I'm willing to do. I always have guard in my game.
– Lamar Odom

I think that's the strength to my game, ... I'm not one-dimensional at all. I'm comfortable wherever he wants me to play on the court. I kind of pride myself being able to play any position. Anything to help us create mismatches, I'm willing to do. I always have guard in my game.
– Lamar Odom

I can't sleep and I can't bathe properly.
– Lamar Odom

We had the opportunity to beat this team by 25-30 points. We didn't because they are well coached and they played hard. We kept doing the little things and got stops when we needed them.
– Lamar Odom

He was saying that I'm learning the role he was five or six years ago. So he understands. The triangle is different. You need four or five guys to understand what's really going on to be effective.
– Lamar Odom

If we play the right way, if we follow our leaders, our coach and Kobe, then we should be a playoff team.
– Lamar Odom

I hope I can keep it going and take it into the playoffs. I'm staying focused throughout the game. I'm trying to do the little things I need to do to win games.
– Lamar Odom

It was fun. We gave them a show. I was glad a lot of the NBA greats came, too.
– Lamar Odom

He's extremely disrespectful. I'm just going to leave it at that. It's dudes like that why things happen off the court between players and their friends and things like that. ... He needs to watch how he talks to other men. There's a difference between competing and how you talk to another man.
Author: Odom Quotes Category: Disrespectful Quotes

They're focusing on defense. You can tell.
Author: Odom Quotes Category: Defense Quotes

It is just game-by-game now. You have to win. My concentration level was high tonight. I've just got an aggressive mind-set right now. I didn't really do anything differently tonight - still rebounded and drove to the hole.
Author: Odom Quotes Category: Concentration Quotes

Don't have a choice right now.
Author: Odom Quotes Category: Choice Quotes

Inside presence, being physical, that's what we need from him. The guy's got the best body in the NBA _ he's got to throw it around a little bit.
Author: Odom Quotes Category: Body Quotes

I take the blame for that (game). I should have ran the clock down more (with 30 seconds left). First time in a long time, my aggressiveness beat me. I was thinking get to the basket. A flop call on a team that is dead, I kind of gave them new life. It's a tough call but I guess it was the right call.
– Lamar Odom

I'll take the blame for that. I should have let the clock run down more. It was a flop call on a team that was dead. I gave them life. He drew the charge, that's what Mr. Crawford saw. It gave them momentum.
– Lamar Odom

Scott Disick Quotes

Whether it is Sir Disick, Lord Disick, or Count Disick, becoming royal is really gonna get the respect that I deserve. Like, I don't need to be walking around like some peasant.
– Scott Disick

To his baby mama Kourtney: Why don't we have the chemistry that Leonardo DiCaprio and Kate Winslet had in Titanic? I'll tell you why: Because we're not in a movie!
– Scott Disick

To his momager-in-law, Kris Jenner: I never realized you were so fun, Jenner. You get drunk during the day, you like to go shopping. I mean, you're right up my alley!
– Scott Disick

I don't mind being portrayed as the villain on TV, but nobody knows the real me. I'm a great guy ... I'm young, handsome, successful, wealthy. You could say I'm a role model. I'm the American dream!
– Scott Disick

When you think of the debonair, ridiculously good-looking guy, you think of me.
– Scott Disick

My great-granddaddy was a pimp.
– Scott Disick

Three thousand dollars for a walking stick? Sounds reasonable.
– Scott Disick

People who say real men don't wear pink obviously don't know any real men!
– Scott Disick

We on a galaxy that haters cannot visit. That's my reality so get off my
– Scott Disick

I can't wait to unleash my fall trend to the world: the walking stick.
– Scott Disick

You don't respect my religion? I don't respect your outfit.
On Rob Kardashian's stint on Dancing with the Stars,

Kid's got moves. I could only imagine him in the sack!
– Scott Disick

I'm kind of a big deal.
– Scott Disick

My hair is flowing in the wind like flocks of Capistrano [swallows].
– Scott Disick

I should make bracelets that say ... What Would Scott
Disick do.
– Scott Disick

I swear, every time [Kourtney] hears me say something
funny, she tweets it and makes pretend she came up
with it.
– Scott Disick

I'm a big star. I don't need to be dealing with you
peasants!
– Scott Disick

I like to work as little as possible to make the most
money.
– Scott Disick

[Kris Jenner has] def threatened to kill me, but who
hasn't?
– Scott Disick

I'm almost human, but not all there.
– Scott Disick

Kanye West Quotes

Kate Upton ain't Marilyn Monroe. Kim is Marilyn Monroe, you know that. She was controversial. She is controversial.
– Kanye West

In my industry, beauty is a talent. You know, 'What is she talented at?' She's talented at being beautiful.
– Kanye West

There's times when I wasn't with [Kim], I wanted to be with her so bad I thought about taking up sports.
– Kanye West

There's no way Kim Kardashian shouldn't be on the cover of Vogue. She's like the most intriguing woman right now. She's got Barbara Walters calling her like every day ... and collectively we're the most influential with clothing. No one is looking at what [President] Obama is wearing. Michelle Obama cannot Instagram a pic like what my girl Instagrammed the other day.
– Kanye West

On turning her into his Barbie doll and making her over: She just needed to be given some platforms of information to work from. One beautiful thing is that as she discovers it, the world discovers it. For her to take that risk in front of the world, it just shows you how much she loves me.

– Kanye West

On how we all just don't get it:
People are so, so dated and not modern. It's like, there's no way Kim Kardashian shouldn't have a star on the Walk of Fame.
– Kanye West

On Barack Obama's criticisms of Kim Kardashian:
He shouldn't mention my baby mama name, 'cause we both from Chicago.
– Kanye West

I remember seeing pictures of her and Paris Hilton in Australia, and I came to Don C., and I was like, 'Man, have you ever seen Kim Kardashian? What's up with Kim Kardashian?'
– Kanye West

I wrote 'Perfect B*tch' about Kim.
– Kanye West

Stop everything you're doing now because baby, you're awesome.
– Kanye West

59468689R00041

Made in the USA
Lexington, KY
05 January 2017